Table Of Contents

INTRODUCTION

My name is Anthony Pham. Right now, my goal is to give something back to all the people who are just like I was. If you are reading this, you probably have at least one job and you work extremely hard at it. You are that one man or woman, among your friends, who is always looking for a better way to get ahead.

Just like me, you feel trapped and let down by a world that promises you rewards if you just work hard. You feel caught up in that 9-to-5 rat race and really don't see a way out. You're tired, frustrated, and broke at the end of each month. I'm here to tell you that there is a better way. It will take some effort on your part, but let's face it, if you went to the trouble of picking up this book, you're not afraid of putting in some extra effort.

Before we start, let me tell you a little about myself. I was born in Boston, Massachusetts. I am a Vietnamese American. My family put a high degree of importance on getting good grades and going to college. I graduated from college with a bachelor's degree in accounting. By age 22, I had my first job as an accountant. I worked hard, getting there early, and staying late. I was doing everything that society tells us to do to be successful.

A few years later, by age 25, I was on my way to earning a Master of Science in Finance. Despite all of this "success," I felt like a failure. How could this be winning? I felt trapped in a cubicle all day. Was this really all there was? I felt lied to and betrayed by a system that repeated the mantra of "get good grades, go to college, get a good job." Well-meaning people in my life drilled that sentiment into me from grade school to graduate school.

I would meet up with friends and they would tell me to "Quit complaining Anthony, at least you've got a good job." I had some of the outward appearances of success. Good job, check. Nice car, check. Good education, check. Despite all this, what I saw was a never-ending treadmill. One where no matter how fast I ran, I never got ahead. I started to do some research. I learned some things that changed my mindset when it came to finances.

With my background in accounting, it was hard for me to accept some of these ideas. I thought I knew it all and I fought back against what this research was trying to teach me. After all, I earned a degree in money, right? Once I was able to open my mind, a world of new possibilities presented themselves. That is something I am going to ask you to do, keep an open mind as you read this book.

This new mindset empowered me to educate myself. I devoured everything I could about personal finance. I read books that taught me about investments, real estate, and the importance of multiple streams of income. I learned from my reading about the importance of leverage. I read books that taught me all about the need to look for positive cash flow. I read books by successful people. These writers were millionaires and I could pick their brains for no more than the cost of a book. It was a bargain.

I used this knowledge to relentlessly apply principles that were not natural for me. Finally, I got out of my comfort zone and took some bold actions. By age 26 I closed on my first rental property, a multi-family building. By 28, I used these principals to leverage my rental income to start another business.

I now have the freedom to walk away from my job if I choose. These businesses now produce more income than my accounting job. Since, they do not take up much of my time, I am going to continue in my job to amass more capital to fund even more business endeavors. Once you have the freedom to walk away any time you want, a job starts to seem like less of a trap.

I want to help you do the same. Our schools do not teach us how to manage our money nor do they teach us how to make our money work for us. We must take matters into our own hands when it comes to our financial education. In the following chapters, I am going to lay out for you, what I did to finally get ahead. If you take the time to apply these principals, your only limitation in how far you can go will be your mind.

CHAPTER 1 - FINANCIALLY EDUCATE YOURSELF FIRST

The first thing I did, and the first thing you will need to do is to increase your financial knowledge. You do not need to go get a university degree on the subject. You do need to be willing to invest by reading books on the subject. I can give you a great overview on the subject and point you in the right direction, but I cannot overcome a lack of financial knowledge for you. You will have to put in the work. If you are not much of a reader, you can invest in seminars and workshops. These really can give you all the education you need. Before you do that let me give you that basic foundation.

The first thing you need to realize is that it is your mind that is your most powerful asset. It is not the size of your bank account. Most people think that to make money you must already have money. Not true. We learn this from our well-meaning parents, friends, and teachers who preach that mantra we talked about earlier. They want you to have security in the form of a "good job." The good news is that all these principals and techniques can work for you while you are keeping the income from your job intact.

Our mind can also be what limits our results. Self-doubt limits all of us. Even the most successful superstars have moments of self-doubt. You need to believe in yourself. The easiest way to overcome these limitations is by educating yourself. When we know what we are doing, our confidence naturally goes up. All one really needs to succeed is some common sense and simple math.

I also need you to really do your best to "get out of your own way." Many of the books I read stressed this point. They had different ways of saying it, but it came down to ridding myself of limiting beliefs. These beliefs have a way of sabotaging your growth and ability to move forward. I read <u>Rich Dad Poor Dad</u> by Robert Kiyosaki. This book helped me break down this idea. We can learn a lot from looking at these beliefs in 5 key areas.

The first is fear. We can be afraid to fail or succeed. We can fear not being smart enough, or not deserving of success. Let me tell you that you need to banish that thought from your brain. You would not be here reading this book if you had anything to truly fear. You are already ahead of so many in the world who let this one thing keep them from pursuing what they genuinely want.

The second is being a cynic. What does it mean to be a cynic? Easy, these are people you know who have all the answers. For example, if you are in a business meeting and you offer a solution, the cynic is the guy that tells everyone all the reasons your idea won't work. You can see how important it is to set aside the cynical part of your brain.

The third is laziness. You must commit yourself to discipline and following through with action. For a long time, I thought of myself as too busy to fit one more thing in my life. I would've told you that I was the opposite of laziness. The trap of "staying busy" is one of the sneakiest ways laziness creeps into our lives. We tell ourselves that we are too busy to take on one more project, but we are just fooling ourselves with bloated to do lists to shield ourselves from the fear of failing at something new.

The fourth is having bad habits. By this I mean, spending our money on things that do not move us forward. I learned by doing my research and reading that rich people buy luxuries last and middle class or poor people are keen to buy them as soon as they can. You may have massive credit card debt, that is a bad habit if the only thing on your statement are clothes you don't need, dinners you could have made at home, and crap that will just end up in a corner unused. You must stop buying things with money you do not have to impress people you do not know. It can be hard to recognize these habits, but they are everywhere. Every dollar you spend aside from the basics, should be on improving your assets not adding to your liabilities.

The fifth and last thing that can hold us back is arrogance. I was certainly guilty of this. When I was educating myself, I would want to argue with the author. Remember, I had that fancy accounting degree. Who were these people to tell me how money worked? I was great with numbers after all. We really must set aside our ego and be ready to learn. Otherwise, you will not receive the maximum benefit from the material. It always drove me crazy when I would go to a weekend finance seminar and see so many people there who just wanted to argue with the person running the event. Why were they there if they were so smart? Why would they waste their money if they were not going to use the information? In a word, ego. They were going to "prove" to themselves how much smarter they were than everyone else. That is arrogance and you must get it out of your personality if you want to move forward.

So what kind of knowledge are you looking for? You will need to educate yourself on the different types of income. We all know that if we go to a job and they give us a paycheck in exchange for our work, we earn an income. We accountants call that type of income "ordinary income." The name even sounds limiting, right? Who wants to be ordinary?

The next type of income is money you earn from investments. You might put extra money into the stock market or real estate. This would form a portfolio of investments.

The last type of income is "passive." Passive income is money that you earn without needing to actively spend all your effort to earn it. For example, you have a business, but other people run it on a day to day basis. The money you collect from that business would be passive income.

To get ahead, I knew that I needed to build income from all three of these areas. I learned that you will not be secure until you have income from more than one source. Job security is a myth in our current economy. Technology is always evolving and making jobs obsolete. The world changes so rapidly that you could find yourself middle-aged and laid off. Now what? If that "secure" job was your only income, you will be in big trouble when the bills come due.

I focused on different ways I could diversify and make money without giving up my job. I looked online for information on how I could earn extra cash from various side hustles. This is something you will definitely want to do. There are many sources available to you online to research these opportunities. One of the best is:
https://www.sidehustlenation.com/ideas/

You can take something that you do as a hobby and monetize it. There are people just like you who are turning their passions into profits. Do not concern yourself with whether it is worth it at this point. You must brainstorm and get all the ideas out of your head. Maybe you are good at photography, is there a way you can earn income from that? The internet is full of folks who need photographs for their content, could you sell to them online?

To give you an idea of a handful of side hustle ideas, I've listed several below to get your imagination and creativity flowing.

Here is a quick list of side hustle ideas to get you started:

- Uber or Lyft Driver
- AirBnB
- Taking Online Surveys
- Blogging
- Child Care
- Baking
- Signing up For Task Rabbit
- Becoming an Amazon Affiliate
- Selling products on E-bay
- Kindle Publishing
- Real Estate Investments-Rental Properties
- Car Wash Service
- Computer Repair Service
- Drop Shipping
- Vending Machines

These are just a few ideas to get you started. The idea is to take something that is easy to learn or that you already know and find a way to earn money doing it.

There are a few things to keep in mind when deciding on something you can do for added income. You will need to decide if you are just looking to make a few bucks or if you want to change your lifestyle completely. There is not a right or wrong answer. If you just want to get into a side hustle to make enough money to pay off your student loans, that's great. It is all about creating options in your life.

These side hustles can qualify you as a business owner. This can be a super complex subject, so we are going to stick to the basics. The plan is not to overwhelm you to a point where you take no action. You must act. What I'm saying is that it doesn't have to be overly complicated. There are so many books on the subject that you will want to read and digest.

As a business owner, you now open yourself to a whole new level of playing the game of life to win. You can now make taxes work for you. Despite what you may be led to believe, the government loves small businesses. As an accountant, I knew from my education and experience that there were so many deductions available to those who ran their own businesses, saving them thousands every year on their taxes.

You will want to make sure that you are getting all the benefits that you qualify for. I will, however, caution you to be careful who you take advice from. Your uncle who once ran a side business out of his back pocket and thinks he can write off his daily bar tab might not be your best source. The point is to educate yourself on the subject and surround yourself with the right people.

Different side hustles have different potentials for changing your financial future. A main criterion I used when figuring out what I wanted to do, was one that I learned from all my research. The successful people I studied created a path for you and me to follow. I learned to focus on how much effort each money-making idea would require from me.

Armed with this knowledge, I looked for ideas that did not need substantial amounts of my personal time and effort. If you must work endless hours at it to generate income you have just turned your business into a job. This was not my goal. Remember my goal was to add options to my life and free myself from the 9-5 world.

I discovered that it was possible to develop ideas into profitable businesses by delegating sizable portions of the day-to-day tasks. I was able to use some creativity to build a team around me that helped me with this goal. I am hoping that this is your goal too. We all have so much potential and you might not believe that you can do it. I challenge you to finish this book and then decide.

So, when I was looking for my side hustles, I was looking for one that I could do after work and on the weekends. I was willing to sacrifice free time, but it had to fit my lifestyle. My job put incredible demands on my time, so I knew that fitting in any added work wouldn't be easy. The plan to use a team of people was appealing but I did not think I could ever make it happen. I didn't have excess piles of cash laying around to pay people. We were supposed to be making more money not spending it, right? With some thinking "outside the box" I was able to put together the help I needed to make this a reality.

I also realized that I needed a business that would produce income. This was my cash flow and managing it was critical to being able to use a team of people to run my business with me. I also knew that I would need to step up my personal organization. I got through college okay. I'm good with numbers and an accountant, so getting organized wasn't too much of a leap for me. I learned that I needed to create systems for my business so that it was easier to run. This allowed me to put certain aspects of the business on auto-pilot. Finally, if I was able to put together a business that grew enough I would need a team. That meant I would have to learn how to manage people.

Ultimately, I chose two side hustles to take my finances and life to the next level. I settled on investing in real estate and running a business that owned ATM cash machines. This seemed to meet my criteria and give me the best chance of winning. It would generate passive income if I did it right. In the next chapter, I will lay out how I started in real estate investing. Then later I will tell you how I started my second business and how I made that fit into my life.

CHAPTER 2 - HOW TO FIND, ANALYZE, AND EVALUATE A RENTAL PROPERTY

Remember, I am an accountant by trade. So, when I looked for a side hustle that would get me out of the rat race, I analyzed all my options. Something that I noticed was that real estate investing was something that most millionaires did. I dug further. Real Estate offered so many advantages. It ticked all the boxes of a great side hustle. Plus, it would not eat up all my free time. The last thing I wanted was something that was just as time consuming as my job. I did not want the number of hours I could invest in my hustle to limit my potential.

Real Estate also had the advantage of offering attractive tax strategies. Taxes and deductions can get complicated. There are whole books dedicated to taxes. I don't want to complicate the story with a drawn-out section on taxes. For now, just know that saving money on taxes is an important advantage of investing and saving money. Saving money was important to me. I wasn't interested in taking in a bunch of money only to have the same amount go back out in expenses. Finally, it made me excited. I genuinely liked looking at property and thinking about: how I would market the property, how it would perform long term, and how it would make me money.

I chose to start with residential real estate because commercial seemed too complicated and sophisticated. It isn't but I was not going to get in over my head when I first started. I also knew that residential property was something that everyone had to have. When I started out, I lacked confidence. I look back now and am amazed at how far I've come. Back then I was just like you. Don't let that lack of confidence hold you back.

You are going to run into people who are going to use a lot of terms and jargon to make themselves seem important. Can real estate investments get complicated? Sure. Just remember that first chapter on educating yourself. You can learn any terms you need to understand. Like I mentioned earlier, you are going to need a team. The world is filled with underpaid experts who can explain it to you in a way you can understand. It took some brutal honesty with myself to realize I too was an underpaid expert. I know more about business accounting than most people. Heck, I know more than the people whose businesses I represented and managed as an accountant. Why were they reaping the rewards while I was willing to accept my wages and trade hours in the cubicle for "security?" Do not let yourself get caught up in this trap of the middle class. The wealthy constantly surround themselves with people who are more talented and smarter than they are in any given area. What sets them apart is the ability to act and to take risks.

When you make real estate your side hustle you can potentially make money in two ways. First, the investment can pay you every month. This is known as positive cash flow. Once you collect all the rent from your tenants and pay off your expenses, the money left over is cash flowing to you.

When real estate investors talk about revenue they just mean the rent paid by tenants. When you look at expenses you are adding up your costs. These include the cost of your mortgage on the property, the amount you set aside for repairs, the amount of any association fees, and any property taxes. You can see why organization is important. It keeps your expenses as low as possible and maximizes your cash flow.

Second, you can realize a profit if the property you buy goes up in value over time. This is what is meant by the term appreciation. Most people in the middle class rely on this strategy for generating wealth. This can be a trap. You will need to be cautious with the advice you get. Well-meaning middle-class people will tell you, "my house is my biggest investment," or "houses always go up in value." I consider this strategy too risky.

We all know stories of people just like us who are let down when the housing market "corrects" itself and gives up large portions of its value. How many people have you heard of that were "underwater" on their personal mortgages? Property appreciation relies on a long-term hold strategy, market timing, and the condition of the economy. This makes it too risky for me when I look at properties to buy. I figure if they go up in value, that is great, more money. If you want to invest in a buy and hold instrument, I'd consider the stock market. It's easier to get out of a stock than a house when things go the wrong direction

Here's the reason I consider cash flow to be king. People always need a place to live. They cannot always qualify for a mortgage, but they can be great renters. Bad economy? I'm not too worried, my renters aren't over leveraged, so they tend to stay. Plus, if I lose one or two, I have people moving down market from homes they can no longer afford, that I can attract. Last, I can reasonably expect to receive the same amount of revenue every month. It is a consistent income.

All of these rely on us choosing the right property. We now have an idea of how it works. I've kept it simple, to press deep into your head that you do not need to make it over complicated to get started. I am here to explain it to you in simple terms and the way I understood it when I started to show you how it can work for you like it worked for me.

So, how do we find the right property? Well first we need to start where the listed properties are listed. We are so fortunate to be able to do this first step online. Can you imagine burning up hours and gas driving around town looking for signs and writing down phone numbers? Here are a few websites that avoid the clutter of individual real estate agents and give you all the information you need:

- https://realtor.com
- https://zillow.com
- https://redfin.com
- https://trulia.com

Out of all the ones above, I prefer Redfin. If it is available in your area, you should give it a try. What I like about Redfin is the way it shows the rental income of the property under the property's details. The drawback to Redfin is that it isn't the best at showing all the MLS listings. You will want to use all the sites to make sure you are capturing all the opportunities available.

You may get some advice from those "cynics" in your life that tell you, "all the good deals are done by insiders, before they ever come to market. You are wasting your time. I'm just trying to help." Something like that will pop up from time to time. Just remember they mean well. You are acting and making them uncomfortable with their own inaction and rationalizations. They are settling for the middle and they want you to do the same. Ignore this advice. I do not concern myself with finding these "off-market" deals and I have done just fine. If you learn of something "off-market" that is a great opportunity, great. But you don't need them to make money and you certainly do not need them to start.

We know where to look for property. What kind of property are we looking for? The first question is do we want single family or multi-family? Single family can be free standing homes, but they may be condominiums or attached townhomes. They have one front door and are occupied by one family. Multi-family has at least two front doors. They are intended for more than one family to occupy. They can be duplexes, small apartment buildings, or large complexes and towers in metropolitan areas.

We want to focus on multi-family for a few reasons. It brings in more cash. This makes it more secure. If we lose one tenant, there is at least one more contributing cash to the business. In single family, if we lose the tenant, we are paying all the expenses out of our own pocket. We want to fund this side hustle using other people's money.

Many advice givers will tell you that there are some real drawbacks with multi-family. First, when we want to sell, we will have a smaller pool of buyers. I don't want you to worry about that. We are not interested in selling or flipping these properties, we are looking for a long-term position and cash flow every month. Cash that will replace the income from our day jobs and give us freedom.

Let me give you an example of what I am talking about, so you can get a feel for what I am talking about. Here are some particulars from a 2-family building I own. This property produces great positive cash flow every month.

The price I paid: $258,000 (sales price)

My down payment: 3% ($7,740)

Monthly mortgage payment: $1400 (monthly expense)

Rental income per unit: $1400 (monthly revenue)

Total Monthly Revenue: $2800

My Monthly Cash Flow

Revenue:	$2800 from rental income
Expenses:	$100 from a coin-op washer/dryer for tenants in basement
	($1400) My mortgage-We accounts put expenses in parenthesis to remind us to subtract that amount.
	($200) water bill and electric bill for common areas of the building
	($300) money I put in a reserve account for repairs and maintenance like lawn mowing or snow removal.
My Net:	$1000 in positive monthly cash flow.

Remember when I told you all you needed was basic math and common sense? This was what I was talking about, all you need is a pen and a pad of paper to figure this stuff out. This also shows the power of multi-family. If I lose a tenant, I still can cover my mortgage with my remaining renter. I can use the security deposit from the lost tenant to repair the unit if needed. I can also use this money to cover the other expenses as well as marketing the property to new renters. Losing both renters is extremely rare. This is why I find small multi-family properties to be more secure.

Let's talk about a straightforward way to evaluate a rental property. Whenever I evaluate a rental property, the most important thing I look at is it's current rental income. I take this amount and compare it to the selling price of the property. A simple way to do this quickly that gives us meaningful results is known as the One Percent Rule. This rule is well known and accepted among seasoned real estate investors. They use it to evaluate many properties quickly.

The One Percent Rule is multiplying the selling price by 1%. If the rental income for the property is greater than 1% of the selling price, the property is worth further evaluation. If not, it's time to move on! Look at the example of my 2-unit property we discussed earlier.

The Sales Price was: $258,000

Apply the One Percent Rule: $258,000 X 1% = $2580

My rental income: $2800

You can see that this property passes the One Percent Rule.

The One Percent Rule should allow you to at least break even. It accounts for all your expenses: maintenance, taxes, utilities, and property management. This rule does assume that the property is in good condition. You can also work the One Percent Rule backwards. Let's say you know the rent. Multiply that number 100 and you have the maximum sales price that the market should support. This can help you negotiate with a seller who has over valued his or her property.

Another thing to consider when evaluating a property is the occupancy of your target. If one of the units is vacant it can be a red flag. You will need to dig a little deeper. Ask yourself why is the apartment vacant? Is there something fundamentally wrong? Will it be hard to attract a new renter?

You also want long-term tenants whenever possible. Is the property in a stable neighborhood? You want the same people in your units because they stabilize your business. Long-term tenants tend to pay on-time, take care of the unit, and make few demands.

You might find a great property that passes the One Percent Rule, but if the building is near a transient area, like a university or college, you are going to have dramatically more turnover. Students tend to move every year and are hard on properties. This can cause your expenses to skyrocket and make the investment not worth all the effort.

If you have a unit that is vacant in the building at time of closing, it is going to cut into your profitability. You will want to consider this when negotiating a deal. Maybe the seller will let you market the unit before closing so you can get someone in there as soon as you close. Or they might be willing to make a concession to you on the price to account for this revenue loss.

One thing I learned early on is not to be afraid to ask. The only thing they can say is "no." Even though you are new to the game, you shouldn't overlook opportunities to make a deal. A real estate agents' number one responsibility is to bring a motivated buyer and seller together.

This does not mean you should go crazy with unreasonable demands. That can quickly cost you a deal on a property you really want. Remember you are the investor, remain calm and professional. Things can get emotional.

This is another reason I prefer multi-family. Investors, like you, tend to own these properties. This means it's usually just business and the deals follow logic. In a single-family deal, you might be dealing with someone selling the family home. A home they consider to be worth more because it has all their memories. After all, they've been living there for the last 30 years. Now anything you ask for can quickly seem like an insult. Now it's emotional and all bets are off.

You can use these simple evaluation tips to make long-term plans. Your new goal should be to work towards financial freedom. You now work at least part-time on your dreams and not your boss's. In my example, I am netting about $1,000 per month. If I need to net $6,000 per month to walk away from my current job. I need to find 5 more properties like the one I already have.

I know this seems obvious. The reason I mention this is to show you that you must look at building things one step at a time. We build wealth incrementally not overnight. Every time you evaluate a property you are one step closer to your goals. Focus on the daily habits of wealth. The results will come if you build the habits.

The end goal will be realized quicker than you think. It is difficult to believe this when you are stuck in the day to day slog. You know the slog that is a job that is demanding, the stress of monthly bills, and the pressure from well-meaning friends and family telling you that you are crazy for stepping off the sidelines and into the game. This life is not just for other people, it is for you too. I was just like you until I wasn't.

You may be wondering about taxes. Yes, you will have to pay taxes on this income. I am sure the experts in your life will have plenty to say about it. Taxation is a complicated subject. There is so much help available on this subject. As an accountant I had the inside track on taxes. So, believe me when I tell you this is manageable. Being a business owner of rental properties has tremendous tax benefits. These benefits are why the rich keep their money and the middle class fund their dreams and the government's programs.

For example, you can depreciate the value of a residential property for 27 and a half years. You can also deduct mortgage interest, property taxes, property insurance and many of your maintenance costs and expenses. When we get to the section on building a team I will remind you to get the right advice. This will allow you to save money on taxes and keep more for yourself legally and ethically.

Our government offers these deductions and benefits to property owners and businesses because it is their investment in our economy that keeps our country growing. We are all doing our own little part to make opportunities for others. That is the benefit of living in a free enterprise economy. The schools I attended never told me this and I am guessing they did not tell you either. This is why we must educate ourselves on how to get out of our current level. Most teachers trapped themselves in a middle-class lifestyle. I say this without judgement. I have many memories of teachers who meant the world to me and helped me tremendously. With rare exception, teachers are not wealthy. They are not positioned to teach us how to build wealth. We must seek this out for ourselves by asking those who have already done what we are trying to do.

One thing that I want to at least mention, is the subject of flipping properties. My strategy relies on the tax advantages of holding property for a longer term. Flipping properties can be a viable business but there are some things that make flipping a little risky for my taste.

There are tax consequences when you sell a property and it goes up in value. The government will force you to pay tax on this appreciation. They call this capital gains tax. You will also be liable for a "recapture tax" for any depreciation of the property you have claimed.

Aside from the tax complications, I am not really interested in flipping houses or properties at this time. I am not willing to put in the constant attention that flipping requires. It can be an expensive learning curve. If you are really set on the idea of flipping properties, I would look at educating myself before I risked any money.

"Great ideas. I get it," you are probably saying to yourself, but you are asking yourself, "How am I going to fund these deals?" In the next chapter we will go over how to pay for a piece of property. So far, we have learned that it is up to us to educate ourselves if we want to break free of the everyday 9-to-5. We have also learned how to find real estate that produces rental income as a side hustle. Take a minute to reflect on how you now have some basic tools to move your life forward financially.

CHAPTER 3 - HOW TO FINANCE YOUR REAL ESTATE PROPERTY

Now that I found a property that met my requirements as a worthwhile investment. It was time to figure out a way to buy it. When real estate investors talk about buying property most want to do it with other people's money. That's good because they've paved the way for people like you and me. We usually do not have enough money in the bank to just write out a check for the purchase price of the property. I knew that I would need some money to use as a down payment to buy this property.

I looked at my bank accounts and all I had was about $10,000 to my name. I don't know about you but that was all the money I had, and it took me a long time to save. Would it be enough? I remembered reading online that most lenders were now looking for buyers to put 20% down. In my example that would have been over $50,000!

I did not have anywhere near the $50,000 but I did have a property that would work. I was frustrated. It was like when you are applying to your first job and everyone is telling you that you need to have experience. How can you get experience if no one will give you your first chance? It was the same thing all over, how was I going to get out of this trap? I needed a property to increase my cashflow, but I couldn't get a property without more money. I did not want to wait any longer, the thought of waiting until I saved up $50,000 did not have any appeal.

I found the answer to my dilemma while doing online research. It's a site I want to share with you. Check out

You will find so many free resources to expand your thinking and knowledge. You can also connect with others just like us, sharing what they've learned. There are free webinars and everything you need to start building a side hustle that moves you closer to financial freedom.

It was on this site that I found an article that explained a technique called house hacking. House hacking is when you live in one unit of a property and the other tenant or tenants pay enough in rent to cover your expenses. You are living rent free. In my case this made perfect sense. It was like being back home and living at my parents. I was able to really cut down on my personal expenses. I was okay with living there the first year. I was new to the game and needed to learn what it was like having tenants and how to deal with everything that being a property owner included.

Plus, I knew from my research on getting property loans or mortgages that it was easier to qualify for a house you occupied. Even better, some lenders would accept as little as 3% for a down payment. In my case that came to about $7,700. I had that much, so far so good. Next, I met with a loan officer at a local bank. He told me that since I was willing to live in the property for a year, I qualified for owner-occupied rates. This was a full percentage point lower than I originally planned. More good news.

I applied for the loan and the lender provided me with an estimate of all the closing costs to the deal. These were expenses that I had heard about and were familiar with from my accounting background. It can seem complicated, but if you break it down, it isn't so bad. Don't let this deter you and derail your plans.

The lender provides you with a document called a "Good Faith Estimate." This lists all the costs that you will pay when buying a property. After my down payment of $7,700, I had about $2,300 left. It wasn't enough to cover the closing costs.

I thought I was out of the game again, but I persevered. I learned from others that there are some creative ways to put deals together. Despite me being a novice investor, I was surprised that lenders, real estate agents, and the online community were there to be an ally in getting a deal done. We came up with a plan to offer more than the list price of $255,000. I ended up paying $258,000. I then asked the seller to rebate me $3,000 which I was able to use to cover the added closing costs I did not have.

Everything went well at closing and I was able to move in. I quickly got familiar with the property. Now I was a new homeowner and a landlord all at once. I knew that it was important to prove myself right away as a credible business person. Plus, there were some improvements that I wanted to make in the first year of living there.

I did not necessarily do all the work myself. I was involved with all the contractors I used and asked a lot of questions. They proved to be extremely helpful when I told them I was a new landlord and was looking to form a long-term relationship with other small businesses that I could trust. I paid them on time and took a lot of their advice.

Many of these repairs and improvements were cosmetic and weren't super expensive. A fresh coat of paint and new carpet went a long way into making the unit more livable. I replaced some old out dated appliances with some new ones. This added more value to the property in the minds of potential renters. This allowed me to ask for rent that was competitive in the market. I did not have to apologize for the condition of the property because I knew I had a rental property people wanted.

That first year quickly passed and I knew it was time to move out and find a rent paying tenant to take my place. This transition was smooth. All my hard work and improvements to the property paid off. It only took me about 2 weeks to find a suitable candidate. They agreed to sign a one-year lease. I now had tenants in both units and the cash started to flow just like my calculations told me they would.

Something I did to show my credibility as an honest landlord was to tell my tenants to call if something went wrong. I made it my rule to get the repair started within 24 hours. My goal was to have long term tenants and not constant expensive turnover. I knew that effective communication and mutual respect was the way to encourage a good business relationship.

Let me give you an example. One my tenants called me to report that their toilet broke and wasn't flushing correctly. A major inconvenience for sure. I called a plumber right away and met him at the property. I really wanted to further my education on my property and show my renters that I was someone who got things done when they called. He told me this toilet was incredibly old and would be difficult to repair. It would be better to just replace it with a new one. I went with his advice. The tenant was happy with the outcome. I was happy, now I won't have to worry about this toilet for years to come. The plumber was happy to work with someone who valued his advice.

This lesson taught me that the previous landlord was short-sighted. He did not keep up on repairs and fought with everyone on how to spend as little as possible. He did not see the big picture. I did not want to lose a tenant. If I lost one, I knew the unit would sit vacant for a month at a minimum. I would be out $1,400 in rental income plus have all the added costs to clean up the unit for the next tenant. This would far exceed an investment in a new toilet.

My tenants are happy with me. I've been lucky enough to have the same two tenants in my 2-family property for the past four years. They tell me that they plan to live here for several years. I have raised the rent twice and each time they were very understanding. I was able to justify these increases by pointing out the improvements I've made. The increase from the city on my property taxes. They are happy with the improvements I've made and know that the market has also gone up. They know that it would cost more for them to find comparable housing somewhere else.

I rarely need to visit the property. We have a relationship based on mutual respect. I know you might be thinking that this sounds involved and time consuming and in the beginning it was. Over time, I developed some systems that allowed me to manage the property without it taking up so much time. We will get to that soon when I teach you how to put together a winning team in the chapter "How to Delegate Your Business."

I've heard multi-millionaires say that the first million was the hardest. They say it gets easier after that. I think it's the same with cash-flow and making investments. I had achieved my goal of profiting from positive cash flow. Even better, that cash flow didn't really take a lot of continual effort on my part.

This was the first step towards financial freedom. I could now breathe easier each month, but I was nowhere near being "financially free."

I felt on top of the world and I was hungry for more. I heard Warren Buffet, one of the richest men in the world, state that the average millionaire had at least 7 sources of income. I knew if I wanted to join this club and get out of the rat race for good, I would need to add more sources of income to my life. Leveling up is the subject of the next chapter. We are going to get into the power of leverage. This will give us the resources to develop those multiple streams of income that are so important to hit our financial goals. I hope that you are starting to feel the excitement that I felt. That you are in control of your life, that you can make positive changes for your future

CHAPTER 4 - THE POWER OF LEVERAGE

We can borrow a term from the gaming industry to explain the power of leverage, "Leveling Up." That is when we get to another level in a game, obviously. What does it mean for you and me when we are trying to escape the rat race?

As I showed you in the last chapter, I was able to build a positive cash flow of $1,000 per month from my two-family property. To say that it would be tough to retire on that income alone is a "no-brainer." To get to the next level, I knew that I needed to buy some more properties.

Buying that first two-family wiped out my savings account. So how was I going to buy another building with limited funds? There were a couple of different ways to approach this. First, I could continue my day job and living my life as normal. I then would be able to bank the $1000 rental income until I saved up enough money to fund the down payment on my next property. This is certainly a workable strategy, but it required patience. I felt like this strategy would limit my ambition to get ahead.

The second way was to use leverage. Leverage is a technique that millionaires use to own lots of properties and businesses without paying out of pocket for them. They borrow other people's money to fund their businesses. President Trump has proclaimed that he is the king of debt. Does this mean he is about to go out of business? Not at all.

President Trump and other wealthy people are where they are because they know the difference between good debt and bad debt. There are many who believe that all debt is bad debt. Some, like Dave Ramsey, state that you should pay off all your debt right away. They say things like "the borrower is a slave to the lender." They base a lot of what they say on simple teachings. These advice givers are equating credit card debt spent on luxuries and things we cannot afford with money borrowed to fund property and business purchases that create cash flow and wealth for us.

I need you to open your mind to the possibility that debt can serve us. We do not have to serve it. When debt is our master we do feel out of control. That's because our behaviors are moving us away from financial freedom. This is bad debt. It is money borrowed to spend on trips we don't need to take, restaurants we should not visit, and other consumer items that do not add value to our lives. I know that many of you think that a vacation to that tropical resort adds value to your life because it allows you to "get away from it all" and reduce stress from your daily grind. However, I will tell you that when the bill from the credit card company comes and you are stuck making payments long after the memory of the fun has faded, you will feel regret and more stress. We want to avoid bad debt at all costs.

Good debt, however, can generate income and increase our net worth. When we borrow money to buy property through a mortgage, we can generate income for ourselves. We already know how to analyze property using tools such as the One Percent Rule. Good debt allows us to use these tools to get more property. Good debt can also fund other businesses, like the ones we will talk about in later chapters.

Some consider loans for education to be good debt and I agree to some extent. What I do not believe in, is borrowing thousands for an education with no real prospect of recouping that money. This seems to be the direction of higher education. I am not trying to open a giant debate in your head. I just want you to think carefully before going down that "go back to school" road blindly. It would be much better to borrow a small amount of money to attend a seminar that gives you the education you need to make 5 times your investment in a short period of time. That is education that I see as worth the investment.

So, I know you are asking yourself, how does this work? A basic definition of leverage for real estate investors is the amount you borrow to finance an investment property compared to its worth. The higher the leverage, or in other words the lower our down payment, the better our potential for a higher return on investment (ROI.)

Return on investment is an accounting term that you should make yourself familiar with. Think of it this way, your ROI is the amount of money made on an investment after you deduct all expenses. Take the amount of money you made and divide it by the total amount of money you invested in the first place, this will give you a number that multiplied by 100 equals the percentage. When investors talk about their investments, they are going to express ROI as a percentage.

You might hear an investor say, "I invested $175,000 in the project and made $26,250 over the next year. It gave me an ROI of 15%." $26,250 divided by the $175,000 invested equals .15. Multiply this number by 100 and you get the figure of 15%.

Let's look at my real-life example to show how down payment and ROI are related. Remember I paid $258,000 for my first two-unit property. Let's breakdown three different scenarios:

Scenario A

If I pay for the property using my own cash to fund the deal, I would own the property free and clear. In simple terms, I write a check to the owner for the $258,000. The property generates rental income of $1,400 per unit per month. This equals $2,800 per month or $33,600 per year. Now I deduct my expenses. Roughly estimating my property tax and property insurance, this equates to $4,200 per year.

Subtracting the $4,200 from the $33,600 leaves me with a new cash flow of $29,400 for the year. Let's assume, for the sake of this example that there are no added repairs or maintenance needed, just to keep it simple. Since I borrowed no money to buy the property, I have no leverage. To calculate my ROI, I take the net cash flow per year and divide it by the purchase price. So, $29,400 divided by the $258,000 multiplied by 100 to get a percentage. In this case that works out to an ROI of 11.4%

Scenario B

I put 20% of the purchase price down and finance the rest. That means that I use $51,600 cash and finance $206,400. I am still generating $33,600 of gross rental income per year. However, my expenses change to reflect the cost of the mortgage. When I add in the cost of the mortgage my yearly expenses rise to $14,400. This leaves me with a net cash flow of $19,200 per year.

Since I put 20% down on the purchase price, I am said to be 80% leveraged on this investment. My 20% down payment represents my total investment of $51,600. Let's look at what that does to my ROI. I take the $19,200 and divide it by the $51,600. This equates to an ROI of 37.20%

Scenario C

I put down 3% of the purchase price or $7,740 and finance $250,260. Again, my yearly rental income is the same at $33,600.

My yearly expenses rise since I am financing more money. Figuring an additional $1,400 per month, the investment is costing me $16,800 per year. This leaves me with $16,800 for my net yearly income. I only put down 3%, so I am 97% leveraged. Using the same method as above to calculate my ROI, leaves me with a 217.05% return on my money.

This shows how putting a smaller amount down can really give your rate of return a boost. I know that we made some simplifications by not including things like maintenance and repairs in our expenses, but this does not change the logic behind the calculations. The larger point is that leverage is a great way to maximize your returns and make it easier for you to buy more investment property.

To tap into this powerful technique, most banks will allow you to use 75% of your rental income to qualify for a mortgage on another property. Different banks have different programs and guidelines. For example, some banks will want to see two years' worth of tax returns. You will need to do some more research to find a bank with a program that fits your situation best. Some banks are more lenient. For example, some will waive the two years of tax returns if you can show a current lease documenting the rental income you receive.

As you buy more property, your rental income will increase. This added income will allow you to systematically buy more property. This is the main concept of leverage and one which wealthy people have been using for years to stay ahead. Now you know this technique too. You can use it to level the playing field and move yourself closer to your goals.

One thing I did learn that I want to share with you on this subject is the concept of debt to income ratio. This is what the banks use to help determine our creditworthiness. The bank will compare the amount of debt you have in relation to the amount of income you receive every month. You need this number to be as low as possible.

There are two ways to improve your debt to income ratio. We can increase our income, or we can reduce our debt. It is easier to pay off debt than it is to increase income. Remember not all debt is equal. Bad debt is the debt that you should be working to eliminate at all costs. This will improve your chances of securing a loan you can use for wealth building.

To get rid of this bad debt, I recommend applying the "debt snowball" technique. This technique was made popular by the same Dave Ramsey we talked about earlier. This is something that I agree with him on completely. If you are trying to pay off debt and ask 5 different people, you are likely to get 5 different conflicting answers as to the best way to do this. The debt snowball keeps it simple and eliminates this confusion.

You can read more about it by simply doing an online search for the term, but I will lay out enough of the plan, so you can apply it. The concept relies on momentum, just like a snowball at the top of a hill. It starts small but as it rolls down the hill it gets bigger and bigger and rolls faster and faster. The same applies to your debt.

The first step is to set aside $1,000 for emergencies. If you do not have that in savings, this becomes the first step. Save $1,000. That way if something comes up, you have the money to pay cash for it and won't tempt yourself to charge it on a credit card. For example, you have a blow-out on the freeway, you now can easily afford to buy a new tire without relying on a credit card.

The next step is to pay the minimum payment on all your credit cards or revolving debt. You then take all the remaining money and use it to pay down the debt with the smallest balance. Once you pay that loan off you turn your focus to the loan with the next smallest balance. You repeat this until you are debt free.

Remember when I said there will be many opinions on this subject? You are going to get pulled in different directions by well-meaning friends, family, or maybe your own pre-conceived ideas. Shouldn't you pay the loans with the highest interest first? No, stick with the smallest loan first. The power of the debt snowball is in its simplicity. This gives you a win relatively quickly when you eliminate one bill from your life and improve your debt to income ratio.

The amount of interest you would save using complex spreadsheets and calculations is not as much as you would think. Dave Ramsey proves every day from his platform on the radio and books that this method is the most effective way to eliminate your debt. We just want to focus on bad debt and open our minds to the wealth building potential of good debt.

We have spent most of this book talking about how to make some money by investing in real estate. In the next chapter I want to explore how we can use some of these same concepts to make money without investing in property. We can use these same ideas to fuel a business that also moves us towards the goal of leaving the rat race.

Let's shift away from the real estate for a bit. I realize that not everyone is going to have a passion for real estate as an investment. It might also be the case that there just isn't a lot of good investment property in your area. Or maybe you are like me and you find the idea of having more than one source of income appealing. Whatever the reason, I want to talk about teaching you how to find other ways to escape the 9-to-5 of modern life.

After I owned my first property for about a year, I made some other changes in my life. I left my corporate job for a different one. I thought the next one would be better but, in the end, it was just the same thing packaged slightly different. That's when I knew I needed to do more to get out of the corporate world once and for all.

I am always looking to educate myself in the areas of wealth and personal development. This desire put the book: <u>The Seven Habits of Highly Effective People</u> by Stephen R. Covey on my list. I am sure many of you may have read it or are, at least, familiar with the title. Out of the 7 habits he mentions the one that got me really motivated was to be "Proactive."

Being proactive, to me, means being responsible for your own outcome in life. There are too many people who take a passive viewpoint and let life happen to them. These are the people in our lives that are always the victim. They are the ones always complaining about how they've been wronged by someone else or were taken advantage of by the system.

This type of attitude always bothered me, but when I read this book, I knew I was guilty of it as well. I was still working at a job that I didn't really love. I tried changing jobs but realized it was the same thing. I was tired of complaining about my life and my job. You know the feeling when you look forward to the weekend starting about Wednesday? By Sunday afternoon you feel that sense of dread, knowing that Monday was right around the corner.

It wasn't that I didn't want to work hard, I just did not like letting other people have that much control over my happiness and my outcome in life. I was no longer going to settle for trading 5 days of work for 2 days of freedom. That's when I started to get really intense and become pro-active about leaving the corporate world for good.

I wanted to find a way to make more money without rearranging my entire lifestyle. That's something I cannot stress enough. When you look for a way to generate income, you must find something that fits you. One size does not fit all in this area. Afterall, if you are shy and not a people person, are you going to enjoy or be successful at a direct sales job.

When considering the possibilities out there we must see ourselves doing it. There is a niche for everyone. Spending some time figuring out our specialty or niche can be the difference between success and failure. We need to find something that is sustainable. All these thoughts were rattling around in my head as I searched for other ways to add to my income.

One day, I was brainstorming about other ways to make money and I kept writing down the term passive income. I knew that I was going to need a way that allowed me to make money without adding too much to my plate. I typed the words "passive income" into Google and studied the list that popped up. One result was "make money with ATM machines."

This caught my attention because I knew the time commitment was something that I could handle. I began to analyze the opportunity to see if it made sense for me. I want to share my experience with an ATM business not because I think it is the only way to make money or even the best way, but because it will give you a great example of how it is not that hard to analyze a business opportunity and to develop a plan to make it a reality.

So, let's talk about what appealed to me about the business. I knew that I could handle the time commitment it would take to run the business. I did not need to be physically at the business for it to generate money. My day job had recently allowed us to work 4 ten-hour days rather than the traditional 5 eight-hour days. This gave me Wednesday and the weekend (if needed) to dedicate to making the business a success.

As we talked about earlier, I knew that most millionaires had multiple streams of income. I thought this would be a way to add some security to my life. That way if the real estate investing slowed down or even if I my employer laid me off, I would have some income to rely on. I shifted my identity to that of a small business acquisition entrepreneur.

It appears everyone you meet wants to be an entrepreneur these days. They are all looking for the next big idea. I knew from being an accountant that most new businesses fail. I also knew from things I read and studied that it can take a long time for a business to make a profit. I was too nervous to invest my time and what little money I had into something that might not even work. I decided that I would look for businesses that were established that I could buy. That is what I mean by the term small business acquisition entrepreneur.

I knew that if I found undervalued businesses, I could make money by applying the same principles that entrepreneurs use with a start-up. I believed that if I found the right opportunities at the right price, I could make money from day one and not have to wait and see if I would get my investment back.

I applied the same sort of analysis that I taught you about real estate to the ATM business. My background as an accountant gave me the skills to look at a business' financial statements. I looked through the statements and calculated a basic ROI. Calculating ROI for a business is really no different than calculating it for a piece of property.

I knew from my background and research that I was looking for a business that generated an ROI of 25% or greater. This is considered good in the business world. With a ROI of 25% I would get all my money back in four years. At first, I was thinking that this was way too long but after those four years I would be making pure profit.

I also knew that I could choose to pay myself from the cashflow of the business if I needed income. It might take me longer to recapture my initial investment, but I would be generating money that I could use every month. Even if it took me longer, I would still be building equity in the business.

Another thing I do when evaluating a business is compare it to my other sources of income. Let's say my hourly rate is $30 at my job and I worked 40 hours per week. I would be earning

$1,200 per week. If I find a business that nets me that same $1,200 per week but only takes me 10 hours per week to run, I am now earning $120 per hour. This would be a major improvement in my life.

Be careful, because the reverse can also happen. Let's say you are generating that same $1,200 from the business but it takes you 60 hours a week or more to run the business, it might not be such a great investment. You might even need to look at brining on a manager to run the business. This would lessen the amount of time you would need to spend on day-to-day operations, but it also lowers the amount of your return.

As you grow, your net worth increases, and your time becomes more valuable. You will need to weigh these decisions carefully. You need to leave enough time in your week to look for new opportunities. One thing I also considered was balance. It is important to look for a business that allows you time to spend with family and loved ones. Remember, we are looking for something that fits our lifestyle.

As I wrap up this chapter, I want to stress that you must find something that interests you. There is a niche for everyone out there. I did not go into the details of my ATM business because I want you to look at all the possibilities out there. It is extremely important to find something that you enjoy and that you can see yourself doing long term.

At its core, evaluating a business comes down to the same fundamentals we explored when talking about real estate investments. I do recognize that it can become a little more complicated when looking at financial statements and balance sheets. I encourage you to invest in yourself by taking a course in business fundamentals. You can learn enough to quickly understand the basic terminology and formulas. This knowledge will give you the confidence to find the information you are looking for when evaluating a business.

Remember, you will want to strongly consider buying an existing business rather than start one from scratch. It is more predictable and there are a lot less surprises. I prefer to acquire businesses because it leaves me with enough time and capital to pursue more opportunities.

I know you are probably wondering about the logistics of all of this. We are going to get into all of that in the next chapter. We will explore the idea of financing a business. We will apply a lot of the ideas that we already know about and also how ROI plays a role in funding our business goals.

For me the niche was buying an ATM business. I am going to stick with my example in this chapter to help explain how I managed to buy an existing business. For you the business might be different, but the ideas will be the same.

The ATM business fit my lifestyle and I had about $14,000 in my bank account. My real estate investments really improved my net worth in just over a year. I was pleased with this accomplishment. This was great because I was not living some bare bones existence. I was not living like some money hoarding cheapskate. I budgeted money to enjoy life, but I wasn't reckless either.

I was not keen on investing my entire savings in a business. Earlier I told you that the goal is to use other people's money whenever possible. I wanted to leverage a small investment to buy things to increase my cash flow.

I found someone with an existing ATM business who was retiring and wanting to sell. I took a cautious approach and asked if he would be willing to sell a few of his machines and the "routes" that went with them. In the ATM business routes are the locations where the machine is located. These agreements are hard to secure, which was another reason I wanted to buy an existing business.

We agreed to a price for the routes. I felt like I got a great deal because my analysis showed that before any financing I would realize a 35% ROI. The seller was happy because he got a fair price for his business and was only selling part of it. This allowed him to make certain that his baby was in good hands.

It was a win-win negotiation which was important to me since I wanted to be able to go back and buy more of his locations when I secured the funds to do so.

My first instinct was to reach out to a bank and apply for a business loan. I learned that business loans are not easy to obtain, especially if you do not have any experience. The bank was asking for a proven track record. They wanted tax records, financial statements, and a business plan. Unfortunately, I had none of those things.

The bank referred me to the Small Business Administration (SBA.) The SBA is an agency of the federal government designed to help small businesses and to encourage the formation of small businesses. The great thing about the SBA is that they provide loans with lower interest rates and longer terms. I found out that an SBA loan was often even harder to qualify for than a traditional bank loan.

They do offer free counseling and advice. This is something that can be beneficial to someone looking to buy or start a business. Advice is given by retired business owners. You definitely will want to explore all that the SBA has to offer. If you can get a loan from them that is just an added bonus.

To buy the business, I ended up taking out an unsecured loan. An unsecured loan is one that is based on the credit of an individual alone. There isn't anything like a house or a car to back the loan. Without this collateral, a bank considers these loans riskier. That is why they tend to have a higher interest rate. This was not an ideal situation and I wanted to quickly find an alternate source of funding.

I needed to get out from under this loan for two reasons. First the interest rate was high and was hurting my ROI. Second, the loan was on my credit report and negatively impacting my debt to income ratio. I needed my debt to income ratio to look as good as possible since I wanted to be able to buy more property once I had the ATM business stabilized.

I did some research on alternate ways to borrow money and settled on the idea of finding a private investor. I read that private investors are more flexible and that you can negotiate everything. They aren't constrained by policies and regulations like a big bank. Finally, private investors do not report to credit bureaus, so any loan from them would not hurt my debt to income ratio.

Before I started looking for investors, I set some ground rules for myself. I did not want to jump at the first offer and get emotionally caught up in this decision. For me it was crucial to find an investor who was looking to be a debt investor and not an equity investor.

An equity investor will loan you money that you have to pay back, plus they expect a percentage of your business. They are loaning you money and the relationship stays after you have paid them back. They will still get their percentage of the profits even after you have paid them back.

Since I planned to hold onto this business long-term, I wasn't willing to share my future growth and profits. That is why I was looking for a debt investor. These investors are just like a private bank, they loan you the money and you pay them back, end of story. The rates on these types of loans are a little higher but that is fair since they are assuming more risk. At the time I bought my business, debt investors were getting between 8 and 10 percent on the money they loan.

Now I had a plan, I just needed to find an investor. This was the hardest part. I knew I was good at analyzing things but reaching out to people to ask for money was something I had never done before. I approached some family and friends to ask them if they wanted to invest. I also used social media to contact people that I knew but weren't in my immediate circle.

There are other ways to meet people that might want to invest. One way is to use the website meetup.com. You can find all kinds of things on this site not just investors. It is great for putting you in contact with people you wouldn't otherwise meet.

Eventually, I found someone who was interested. It turned out to be someone I knew since high school who I hadn't really kept in contact with over the years. It turned out he was successful and always looking for new business opportunities. We set up a meeting and he told me that he was extremely interested. Then he asked me for my business plan and financial statements. My heart sank, he was just like the bank.

When he told me this, I was like business plan? I had never written one before and I was unorganized with my financial statements. I was determined. I wrote out a simple plan of how the business performed and how I proposed to pay back the money. I went back to the seller and asked for copies of his records for the previous year. I had 3 months of my own bank records plus the previous owner's. They all showed similar cash flow.

I took my records, my basic plan, and added my agreements that secured the right to have the ATM machine in the locations I bought and assembled them into a portfolio. I was now ready to meet with my investor again. Depending on what type of business you buy, you may need other documents. The point is that you need to be as prepared as possible and present an organized plan.

Do not let a lack of experience hold you back, investors are just people. If you can make the deal make sense to them, there is a good chance they will invest. Do not worry about knowing all the right terms. Just speak to them in your own words and be prepared to answer their questions about how you are going to pay them back.

Armed with my portfolio, I made my pitch. My investor was still interested, and he initially wanted to buy half of the business. I stuck to my guns and said I wasn't looking for an equity partner. This was harder to do than I thought. I was worried that he might pull out all together. Ultimately, I offered him a rate of 8.5%. He was happy to have a source of income that needed no effort on his part, passive income.

I ended up using the money from this loan to buy more ATM routes. Over time, our relationship became stronger and he trusted me. I borrowed more money from him to pay off the unsecured loan that I initially took out to buy those first routes. I learned a ton from my first investor and set a goal to become an investor myself when I built up more wealth. To have that type of passive income is very appealing to me and I hope it becomes one of your long-term goals as well.

My business grew, and I developed a good reputation in the field among hosts. Hosts in the ATM business are the businesses or people who own the locations where you want to place your ATM machine. I used a system to run my ATM business that was consistent and delivered a machine that was consistently up and running. This was important since they are the ones that deal with angry customers when the machine is down.

This good reputation and my discipline to always keep looking for more led to another opportunity to buy more ATM locations. I decided to use another private investor. I wanted to stay diverse and build another relationship. My experience with my original private investor paid off, this time around it was much easier.

I had two private sources for money. I was on a streak and able to use some velocity and momentum to build up a great business. You can apply these same techniques to your life. It doesn't have to be the ATM business. I had a lot of self-doubt when I started but I refused to let it stop me. I did my research and educated myself, this built up my confidence.

You need to have confidence in yourself and in your business or nobody else will. Confidence is one of the biggest factors that private investors consider when they make decisions. Don't get me wrong the bottom line is important too, but if you don't believe in what you are doing, neither will they.

Over the next year, I bought multiple routes, most of them small, but they added up to a substantial business. I now had enough cash flowing monthly to replace my day job. With all this going on you are probably wondering if I sleep or how I fit all of this into my daily life without feeling burned out and running around like a crazy person. I consider myself an efficient person by nature and I developed systems to run my businesses.

I also delegate portions of my business to other people to free up time for me. I can do whatever I want with this time. For me, I try to strike a balance between a fun lifestyle and being vigilant in my search for more business opportunities. In the next chapter, I will teach you how to delegate your business, so it does not take over your life.

I am going to share my experiences with you to show you that you can learn how to become more efficient and less overwhelmed when your businesses begin to really take off. I made some mistakes and learned a lot by trial and error.

By learning from my mistakes, you can save yourself a bunch of pain. Some of these examples might help you directly, but the lesson they teach is more important. Use these examples to think critically about your own unique circumstances and see how you can apply them to make your life easier.

As the ATM business really took off, my stress levels went through the roof. I was spending 60 to 70 hours per week trying to do everything myself. I was working 40 hours every week at my day job. The good thing was that I worked those four ten-hour days and had Wednesdays off. This gave me time to really work on my side hustles. My growing ATM business was eating up almost twenty hours a week and then the rental property made demands on my time.

I knew there was a better way. I looked for ways to streamline my rental property's demand. One thing I eliminated was collecting rent checks in person. On the first of every month I used to make the twenty-minute drive to my building, knock on the door, and ask for the rent. This was not efficient at all. If the tenant wasn't home or did not have the rent at that moment I would have to return later.

I met with my tenants and asked them to help me come up with a workable solution. We discussed that they could mail the checks to me, but the mail takes too long, and I did not want to get stuck with the excuse "the check is in the mail."

Eventually, we came up with a way for them to deposit their rent directly into my account. They could pay me on time, when it was convenient for them. There were no checks to write out for them and there was no time wasted on my end, going to the bank to make the deposit. This system saved me a couple of hours per month.

The property was also eating up my time with maintenance. If you remember back to the beginning of our journey, I lived in this property for the first year. I was used to doing the lawn mowing and snow removal myself. It wasn't a big deal since I lived there. Now I was making that twenty-minute drive every time it snowed. In the summer it was even worse, I would be there at least twice a month to mow the lawn. In the fall, I would spend entire Saturdays there, raking leaves that fell off a giant tree in the backyard.

Again, my tenants supplied some creative solutions. One of my tenants worked for a landscaping company. In the winter they did snow removal. He was able to take care of any snow removal for a $50 rent credit. This same tenant also mowed the lawn in the summer for only $25 per cut. This was far better than hiring a landscaping company. I offered a $100 rent credit to the other tenant to take care of the fall leaves. Everyone was happy.

I know that not everyone is going to have tenants like mine, but the point is to be creative with your solutions. My rental property went from being a drain on my time to running on auto-pilot. I also stopped making all the basic repairs myself. I found a handyman on Angie's List. Over the years, we have developed a great working relationship. He knows that I pay on time and he does great work. If something major goes wrong, I call in the right people. For example, my sump pump broke one time and rather than let my handyman get in over his head, I called a plumber.

Angie's List is a great resource. It is subscription based, the current fee is $25 per year, but it is well worth every penny. You can use it to read reviews and only hire reputable contractors that do the work they promise to do.

This system of delegation worked great for me. I was solving my problems creatively. I was only paying for services when I needed them. Property management firms wanted a monthly fee every month even if they didn't have to do anything. Landscaping companies worked the same way. They wanted a guaranteed amount per month, even if the snow did not fall or when the grass grows slowly at the end of the season. I did not want a monthly drain on my cash flow if I could help it.

This is what I mean when I talk about building a team. Property management and landscaping companies are not the only way of delegating a real estate business. Thinking outside the box allowed me to surround myself with a team without formally hiring anyone.

There were other benefits to going this route as well. Having my tenants help with the seasonal maintenance also meant that the people living there were doing the work. I knew they would do a respectable job and do the work when it was needed. I did not want to hire a management firm that I would end up managing.

The ATM business was really eating up my time too. Especially when I first started, everything was new to me. My transition was as smooth as it could be, the previous owner did what he could to ensure that I would be successful. However, there were things that would go wrong from time to time. I didn't know as much about the function of the machines as I should've. I am admittedly not very handy, so it wasn't easy for me to figure all this out.

I was definitely getting my education in the ATM business. Sometimes my machines would run out of money during special events that I didn't know about. I knew that I could not have this kind of customer service let down. The first summer in the ATM business was crazy.

I woke up every day at 5 AM to run around and service my machines before work. Many of my machines were in hotels that were far busier in the summer. They needed service at least every other day. I would service them, then go to work. I often used my lunch hour to go to the bank and get the cash I needed to replenish the machines. The trip to the bank would take a full hour because I was waiting in line and withdrawing a significant amount of money.

After my ten-hour day of accounting, I would make the one-hour commute home. By the time I got home it was usually around 8 PM. Then I would wake up and do it all again the next day. My life was like the label on a shampoo bottle: lather, rinse, repeat.

I knew this was crazy and not realistic to keep up long-term. There were times when I felt like giving up. I would ask myself, "What did I get myself into?" But, I refused to give up and let a little bit of overwhelm stop me. You are going to go through this as well. Do not let these feelings stop you. Keep moving forward. The path to success isn't all that complicated but nobody said it was going to be easy.

I began to see some patterns and ways I could make the ATM business fit into my life a little better. I knew I needed to build better relationships with the people I met on a regular basis. Just like my real estate properties, I needed good relationships to make the business operate smoother and be easier to run.

This led to me changing banks. I found one that was smaller and prided itself on customer service. I met the branch manager who introduced me to everyone. I explained to her what my business needed. We worked out a system where I could call ahead and request the funds I needed to withdraw. Now when I got to the bank, everything was ready, everyone knew me, and I was in and out in a few minutes.

I also went to all my locations and met with the people in charge. Many of my locations were in hotels. I asked them about special events in the area and in their hotels that would affect my machines. Once we got to know each other, we worked out a system that ensured that I knew when a big event was in town. Lots of the larger hotels also allowed me to valet my car and get in and out quickly. This all saved me time, allowed me to improve customer service, and cultivate great business relationships.

These improvements helped me free up time to market my ATM business. I looked for better more profitable locations. I targeted locations that were near my other accounts or by my day job. That made it more efficient and I was able to market my services while I was in the area anyways.

I learned from my experience with my tenants that life was better when I stopped trying to do everything myself. I decided to start small and begin to add to my team to help me grow. I hired an independent contractor to help with the bookkeeping. This may seem odd coming from an accountant, but I knew how time consuming this task can be. As I grew, I knew my time would continue to become more valuable. I had to figure out a way to free up time to do the tasks that were the most profitable. I used the bookkeeper to leverage my time, just like I was using loans to leverage my money.

As I continue to buy up ATM routes, I will look soon need to hire someone as an independent contractor to service the routes. For now, I have invested the time to make my systems efficient enough that if I plan ahead I can service my locations without too much trouble. I service ones convenient to my office during the week and use Wednesdays to take care of everything else.

I have dreams to build my business even bigger. I meet with a business broker regularly who looks out for opportunities he thinks will fit my investment criteria. The most important thing here is that I make plans for my dreams. I give them deadlines. This is what turns them into goals and keeps them from remaining dreams that someday may or may not come true.

There wasn't too much I could change about my full-time job to make it less demanding. My job was already pretty flexible and gave me Wednesdays off. The hour long commute each way was not ideal. Since I no longer needed the job to survive I was able to negotiate with my employer from a position of strength. We worked out a deal where I would work from home on Fridays. This was great because the two hours I save commuting can be used for something more productive.

Now that I am what I call an acquisition entrepreneur, I've learned to surround myself with the right people. This is important for you to implement sooner than you think. You are going to have to put in the time and effort to build a business but do not allow that "busy-ness" to limit your business.

Being successful in business depends on the relationships you build and the reputation you develop. This chapter should show you how important it is to build good relationships with everyone you can. If you only look out for yourself, you will be limited by what you can personally and physically do. Harnessing the power of a team can get you to a much higher level.

CHAPTER 8 - CONCLUSION, PUTTING IT TOGETHER AND WHAT TO DO NEXT

It's been over a year since I bought my first ATM business. I've made a total of three acquisitions to grow my business so far and I'm not looking back. As I stated before, I no longer need the income from my day job. I am in a position to walk away from it if I want. My cash flow from my businesses was enough to free me from the rat race.

Once I realized that I did not have to be there, the job did not seem so bad. It provided me with extra income that I could use to further invest and get ahead. I know that I will eventually have to give up the job as my time becomes more valuable and better spent looking at more opportunities.

I plan to remain as long as I can, until I can't juggle everything. My original goal was to escape the grind of the daily 9-to-5, but now I've set my sights higher. That's the funny thing about goals, you never really arrive. Once you achieve one, your mind looks for the next thing to accomplish.

I set my new goal to be financially free. This can mean different things to different people. For me, I want to be able to live life on my terms. I want to have enough sources of income that I am not dependent on any one of them to fuel my lifestyle.

Only you can decide on your goals. The most important thing is to truly ask yourself what you want out of life. You may love your job, maybe it is your passion, but you want to build an investment income to give you a sense of security. Your goal could be to retire early or to change careers without fear. It is important that your goal be something that motivates you. Watch out for the trap of adopting other people's goals. It is hard to commit yourself to something that you do not fully desire or believe in.

Another thing about goals that I learned and want to share with you is to write everything down. For example, it is not enough to say that you want to retire early. Write it down and answer the specific questions about your goal. How much will you need to generate in monthly cash flow to replace your income? When will you achieve this?

From there you can break it down into smaller to manage day to day tasks. That way it will be easier to stay on track. You will have a sense of urgency to work on your life every day.

Lots of people say they want to become rich or that they dream of walking away from it all, but they never take any action to get there. When you run into these people later in life, they are still talking about the same vague dreams that they hope will happen someday.

You would have a better chance winning the lottery than following their recipe for life. You need to be specific and act. I wrote this book not to brag about how much I've done with my life but to show you what you can accomplish in a short period of time with a little common sense and basic math.

Do not let excuses hold you back. The time will never be perfect to get started. You aren't too young or too old. I did not listen to doubters in my life who kept telling me the reasons why this would not work. I listened to my own heart and drive that told me I could do this if I just kept at it. I sought out people who had already done what I wanted and modeled their behavior. And you know what? So far it has worked, and it can work for you too.

Now one chapter in my life is ending. I am no longer chained to my cubicle and dreading every Monday. A new chapter is beginning for me. I am looking at taking the next step to level up my life. I want to achieve financial freedom. I hope that you enjoyed reading about my journey. I hope that you found value in the information I shared in this book.

Moving forward, I am dedicated to continue sharing my story. I hope you will join me in future books as I talk about the steps I take to get to the next level. I wish you success in your individual lives and hope that your experiences are as life changing as mine have been.

Thanks Again,

Anthony Pham